**Beyond the Rules is published in the United States by X60 MEDIA, LLC**

## © 2010 by X60 MEDIA, LLC
All rights reserved.

## Created by Al Battista, Tim Malloy, and Billy Martin

For Official /Umpire resources, visit:
## www.ref60.com

Necessary corrections and subsequent updates can be found at:
## www.beyondtherules.net

ISBN 978-1456510015
First Printing: August 2010

# Table of Contents

# Forward

**N**o matter what the vocation or endeavor, it is the people who go beyond what is expected of them who ultimately achieve the loftiest goals.

The standards for excellence sit on a much higher plane than the benchmarks for competency, and everyone makes a choice, either consciously or by default, the path they will travel.

Now if you decide you are willing to pay the price for greatness, no matter what the field, it will require a vigilant effort to make sure your daily deeds align with your stated intentions.

As a basketball official, if you have chosen to walk the road less traveled, then *Beyond the Rules* will be an invaluable guidebook on your journey to maximizing your officiating abilities and experiences.

This book will also be an insightful read for conscientious basketball coaches and players who are looking for a better understanding of how the game is officiated, as well as fans looking to enhance their basketball viewing experience.

*Beyond the Rules* is a full-access backstage pass for players, coaches and spectators into the thought process and preparation of officials who will be managing their future games.

While a firm grasp of the rules is an absolute necessity for any level of officiating success, it is getting **beyond the rules** where the image of difference lies in making meaningful progress in such a competitive avocation.

Getting **beyond the rules** and immersing oneself in the intangibles of game preparation and game management, as well as gaining a deeper understanding of the sophisticated techniques for better court coverage, will make an official more in-demand with assignors, fellow officials, coaches and more respected and appreciated by spectators.

So read and dream **beyond the rules** and take your officiating career, and your basketball experience, farther than you ever thought possible...

Al Battista,
Tim Malloy,
and Billy Martin

# About the Authors

Al Battista is first and foremost an educato and his passion for basketball officiating a his desire to share his in-depth knowledge on the subject has been utilized at all levels of the game.

Al is a 33-year respected member of IAABO and a dual member of Board 215 (West Virginia) and Board 12 (Washington D.C.), and currently serves with distinction in the high school and college ranks as the Interpreter for the West Virginia Intercollegiate Athletic Conference (WVIAC), the Pennsylvania State Athletic Conference (PSAC), the Capital Athletic Conference (CAC), the Maryland Junior College Conference, and is on the IAABO Rules Examination Committee. In the professional game, Al has been a staff observer for the NBA and WNBA since 2004 and 2007, respectively.

Al also is the creator and editor of the highly-respected officiating newsletter, MATCH UP and was on staff with the MEAC for 26 years while earning three "Sweet 16" round assignments in the NCAA Division III tournament. Al currently is a member of CBOA and the Big South Staff.

*Contact Al Battista via email:*
*albattista12@comcast.net*

# About the Authors

Tim Malloy, between the ebb and flow of a chronic illness that has required 32 surgeries, has pushed forward and carved a path of distinction in both the world of basketball and business.

As a 37-year veteran referee of IAABO Board 34, Tim has worked numerous New Jersey state playoff games and climbed the ladder to the college ranks. Tim officiated as a member of CBOA where he earned Division II and III playoff assignments.

Off the court, Tim was a front office executive for the NBA World Champion Philadelphia 76ers in 1983 and served as the team's Assistant Group Sales Director and Public Relations Director for seven seasons. Tim later worked as a Sales and Promotions representative for Converse Inc., where he was a two-time Salesman-of-the Year award winner. He also holds a U.S. Patent for a golf training device that received a 4-star rating in Golf Magazine and is the co-author of the sports reference books, *Blue Book 60* for fast pitch softball and basketball.

Tim is a graduate of St. Joseph's University (PA) and resides in Somerdale, NJ with his wife Pattie, son Matt and daughter Mary Frances.

*Contact Tim Malloy via email:*
*board34@comcast.net*

# About the Authors

**B**illy Martin has over 30 years basketball officiating experience for IAABO Board 34 in Camden, New Jersey.

He currently serves as the Supervisor of Officials for the 300-member organization and is responsible for official's ratings and education.

In the business world, Billy has more than 27 years of sales and marketing experience, and currently works with Salesforce.com, the industry leader in Customer Relationship Management tools.

Billy holds a Master's Degree in Education (MEd) from The College of New Jersey specializing in Sports Medicine and a Master's Degree in Business Administration (MBA) from the University of Phoenix in Technology Management.

Additionally, Billy is a scholastic fast-pitch softball umpire for the NJSIAA (West NJ Chapter #5) along with USSSA New Jersey. He is the co-author of the widely respected rules education book titled, *Blue Book 60- Fast Pitch Edition* which can be found at www.bluebook60.com.

Billy resides in Mt. Laurel, NJ with his three daughters, Jennifer, Jessica, and Alissa.

*Contact Billy Martin via email:*
*billymartin@comcast.net*

# References

Please refer directly to the official rule sets for each organization, as this publication is intended to go **beyond the rules** and not replace the official publications of these associations.

## (NFHS) -- National Federation of State High School Associations

The NFHS, from its offices in Indianapolis, Indiana, serves its 50- member state high school athletic/activity associations, plus the District of Columbia. The NFHS publishes playing rules in 16 sports for boys and girls reaching 18,500 high schools and over 11 million students involved in athletic and activity programs.

*NFHS Publications Order Department – www.nfhs.org*
*P.O. Box 361246*
*Indianapolis, IN 46236-5324*
*Phone: (800) 776–3462*

## (NCAA) -- The National Collegiate Athletic Association

The National Collegiate Athletic Association (NCAA) is a voluntary organization through which the nation's colleges and universities govern their athletics programs.

*NCAA Publications Online – www.ncaapublications.com*
*P.O. Box 6222*
*Indianapolis, Indiana 46206-6222*
*Phone: (317) 917-6222*

# Personal & Partner Pre-Game Pointers

The goal of every word in every chapter of **Beyond the Rules** is to offer meaningful "sword sharpening" techniques for officials to incorporate into their game that will deliver the improvements they desire.

To that end, the **Pre-Game Pointers** checklist below is to serve as an outline that will improve your personal accountability on the court, as well as provide coverage clarity with your officiating partners.

## *Personal Pointers*

- Know your shooter on all fouls requiring free throws.
- Know the number of free throws made on each pair of attempts.
- Straight arm chop and count on throw in.
- During a dead ball, hold the ball; don't play with it.
- Be aware of your posture – stand straight and keep your chin up.
- No hands on hips or arms crossed.
- Be aware of your facial expressions.
- Know the time, score and fouls on every whistle.

## Working (or Transitioning to) the Lead

- Don't get beat back down the floor.
- Stay WIDE on rebounds.
- Keep a patient whistle.
- Focus on strong side rebounding.
- Take a glance at game & shot clocks.

## Working (or Transitioning to) the Center

- Don't leave too soon.
  Stay to help with pressure.
- Proper free throw positioning (NFHS & NCAA Men's vs. NCAA Women's)
- Look for fouls on spin moves inside.
- Observe players slashing through the lane.
- Concentrate on weak side rebounding plays.
- Take a glance at game & shot clocks.

## Working (or Transitioning to) the Trail

- Keep a "big picture" mentality.
- Stay off the floor until the ball is inbounded.
- Monitor all rebounding plays.
- Take a glance at game & shot clocks.

## Partner Pointers

- First call sets the tone; make it a good one.
- Call what you see, and see what you call. No guessing.
- Player Control fouls – make sure offense is "to and thru" the defender.

## *Foul Absolutes*

- If dribbler's rhythm, speed, balance and quickness is affected.
- Two hands on dribbler.
- Dribbler falls down by contact.
- Contact on rebounds, if possession is affected. Or to clean up play.

## *3-Person Crew*

- Look for reasons to rotate.
- Find the key matchup(s).
- Ensure strong side officiating.
- Get Lead & Trail on ball side.

## *Travelling*

- Find the pivot foot.
- Unless you're certain, don't call it. Be certain.

## *Miscellaneous Game Management*

- For injured players, call the coach/athletic trainer, and then move away from the scene.
- Always take proper positions during time outs.
- Referee the defense while making sure the offense is legal.
- Keep a patient whistle in the Lead, and an active whistle in Center & Trail.
- Let plays develop and finish below the FT line. Don't penalize a good move.
- Stay connected to the plays originating in your matchup area until completed.
- Let your feet follow your eyes.
- Keep active feet – move for open angles.
- Come together for flagrant, technical and intentional fouls.

- Note the style of play of the two teams.
- Note coaches' attitude towards officials – strategy for aggressive coach?
- Note any crew history with a coach or player.
- Note any team history – rival game or any bad blood.
- Determine the competency level of the table crew.
- Be aware of overzealous spectators.
- Be aware of any safety issues with cheerleaders or spectators.

Work all or some of these points into your personal pre-game, and into your crew discussion before tipoff, and you will find yourself moving confidently and competently forward on your officiating career path.

# Sanctity of the Locker Room

The phrase, *"respect the burden,"* was offered by the noted French General Napoleon Bonaparte as a succinct reminder to the masses and the well-intended to not impede the duties of those tasked with a heavy responsibility.

All officials would be greatly served by General Bonaparte's credo if friends, loved ones and colleagues were made more mindful of the importance of preparing for the game task at hand and the locker room boundaries before, during and after the contest.

The quality and size of the dressing room facilities provided for officials varies from school to school, but regardless of the aesthetics, a certain protocol should be adhered to for the benefit of the working officials.

> **Is this area really the place for a pre-game social call or a halftime pop-in visit by well-intended fellow officials?**

Are these confines the appropriate spot for an officiating crew's friends and family to gather immediately after the game?

There is no doubt a sensitivity of finding the balance between enjoying the company of your colleagues, and doing what is necessary to **"prepare-correct-and assess"** for every assignment in your pre-game, halftime and post-game rituals.

## *Pregame*

If you're coming to watch a game, chances are your arrival time is after the working officials have already begun their pre-game stretching and conference, so a pop-in visit to offer your best wishes is discouraged.

If you are a new official and would like to observe a respected veteran's pre-game; by all means ask if you can sit in, provided you can make this arrangement before the officials have gone to the dressing area. However, this is not the time or place for questions. Make mental notes to follow up sometime after the game with any questions.

## *Halftime*

While there can be a healthy discussion on the true impact of peer visitors prior to the game ...

> **The locker room at intermission should be the exclusive domain of the working officials.**

There is a very limited time to discuss any first half issues and second-half strategies, and officials need to be able to maximize these few minutes with an open exchange with their partner(s). This is a conversation that would likely be stifled with an uninvited guest.

If you would like to stop in the locker room to extend congratulations to the crew for a well officiated game, please wait 10-15 minutes for the officials to decompress and share their postgame thoughts with each other.

Especially, if it was a game with some added drama or controversy, the officials will no doubt appreciate the privacy extended to them. You may even decide against making an appearance.

Put yourself in the working officials' position. Would you feel like socializing after this game? If the answer is, "no," then skip the post-game visit.

In that vein, please be mindful of your comments to the crew, and frame them in a manner that is supportive and helpful.

So no matter the size, condition or its location ...

**The official's locker room is to be a buffer zone from the biases and criticisms of the players, coaches and fans.**

Make sure you respect the boundary lines of this sports sanctuary, and give your fellow officials the privacy they need to prepare, correct and assess for each game.

They will appreciate being spared the awkwardness of having to ask for something they are entitled to, and you will no doubt be extended the same courtesy for the games you officiate. And in the words of Napoleon, *'respect the burden.'*

# Referee in Small Bites

There is an old African proverb that asks the question, 'how do you eat an elephant?' and the answer is, 'one bite at a time.'

The point of the "small but steady" approach to polishing off a pachyderm is a philosophy that can also be applied to the task of officiating a basketball game.

**Breaking a 32-minute high school game or 40-minute college clash into smaller more manageable two-minute "bites" can reduce your pre-game stress level and build confidence as your game goes along.**

There is a grain of truth in a coach's joking remark of wanting perfection at the start of every game and for the officials to get better as the game goes along!

This "two-minute approach" can help you deliver what they are demanding.

Striving for perfection in a 32 or 40 minute game may be an unrealistic goal, but a more manageable objective of error-free officiating for two minutes, is something that is certainly achievable.

The key is to string as many two-minute clips together as possible.

Toss the ball to start the game and focus on getting two minutes down the road. Set the bar for fouls and violations at a level you can consistently adhere to throughout the contest. Focus on managing only the player activity in your primary area and be conscious of not encroaching into your partner's area of responsibility.

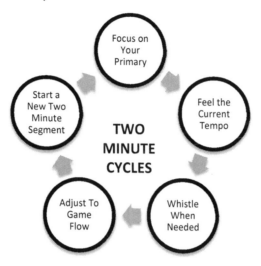

*Diagram: Two Minute Cycles of Concentration*

Again, the notion of small servings – in terms of time as well as area of coverage – will serve you well in the long run.

And after a handful of 120-second segments, you will be at halftime and ready to take on the back end of your basketball beast. Now should you or your partner(s) have any 'hiccups' in one of your 2-minute mini-games, you simply mentally pardon yourself and resume your pursuit of perfection.

# Freedom of Movement and Setting the Tone

**T**he United Nations General Assembly in 1948 established the Universal Declaration of Human Rights that unequivocally proclaims the fundamental right of freedom of movement for all people.

Certainly the game of basketball would defer to the importance of the document championing the global expression of human rights, but the powers that govern our game have made 'freedom of movement' a critical point of emphasis to enhance the natural offensive flow by limiting the overly physical pressure applied by teams at the defensive end of the floor.

> **Players and coaches will be looking to see what type of tone the officiating crew will set for the game at hand, and they will react accordingly**.

This means today's officials are challenged to quickly and consistently distinguish between:

- Contact that is incidental and marginal and ...
- Contact that is overly aggressive and illegal.

Incidental and marginal contact is that which is practically unavoidable when 10 players are put in the confines of a normal size court and freedom of movement is not affected. This also is contact that you have determined through constant and instantaneous evaluation is not gaining an illegal advantage by the perpetrating player.

However, contact that is deemed to be displacing a player from their intended path or is preventing a player's freedom of movement is to be ruled a foul and should be called immediately and consistently.

Bumping or holding an offensive player attempting to cut through the lane left unchecked will undoubtedly turn the game into something resembling a rugby scrum.

A watchful eye also needs to be kept for overly aggressive play that can very quickly escalate into a heated exchange between players that could warrant intentional fouls and ejections from the game.

Players for the most part, are not looking to fight, but they will resort to defending themselves if they feel the officials are not going to protect them from illegal and overly aggressive play. Shoves, elbows, clutches, jersey grabbing and punches are normally in retaliation to a frustrated player being subjected to the same type of contact with no relief being offered by the officials.

A firm but fair officiating approach will keep players from feeling they must mete out their own form of on-court justice, and also will quickly penalize the instigating incident while quashing the notion of players 'sending a message' with overly aggressive contact that is meant to intimidate the opponent.

**Setting the tone for the game is not just limited to the type and frequency of foul rulings, but also for violations.**

In addition to ruling early and decisively on illegal screen and hand checks, officials would be wise to clean up at the outset abuses of offensive players clogging the lane for more than three seconds, and for taking liberties with their pivot foot and illegal dribbles.

Manage each game with a goal to set a tone from the outset that is fair and consistent, and promotes freedom of movement, and you will likely find yourself in a contest where the players will adjust and it will be skills and execution that will determine the outcome of your games.

# Why Do Officials Miss Plays?

**W**hen the subject of why officials miss plays is discussed, being out of position is the culprit most often offered up as the cause. But officials who are dedicated to sharpening their skills should also consider their balance, mental preparation and conditioning as credible reasons for on-court mistakes.

**Indeed, officiating in a parked position and "standing on a dime" will no doubt hinder an official's performance and judgment.**

You certainly need active feet to keep from becoming an official who is guessing on many plays during the game.

Don't fall into the trap of standing still and officiating like a commander staring through a periscope and peeking around corners. Know where to be, based on the game action, and work to get there so you can officiate the play with your eyes, and not rely on your guile, savvy and instinct.

**Emphasize <u>balance</u> as a critical component for getting plays right.**

The weight of the official working in the **Lead** position should to be on their **back foot closest to the basket** in a staggered stance. This back foot is typically closest toward the basket providing a boxed in viewing angle.

Staggering your stance will assist with maintaining a patient demeanor and letting the play develop in front of you as the Lead official.

Weight Distribution as Lead in the Preferred Staggered Stance

Another factor in booting calls is the official being surprised by the play. The offensive player makes a move or the defender makes a play the official is not prepared for, and is out of position. So the official mentally flips the proverbial coin.

But had the official invested their pre-game time wisely and closely observed the players warming up, the official might not have been caught flat-footed.

> **Officials should identify through simple observation the better players who will likely earn the most minutes of a close game.**

Find the shooters and watch their form. Do they take an illegal "bunny-hop" before they release the ball? If so, be ready for when that player catches a quick swing pass and then takes a step before releasing the ball.

Do they kick out their leg as they go up and return to the floor? If so, be on guard for when that player "crashes" to the floor from the contact they initiate with a legal defender.

Find the ball handlers and watch their moves. Do they palm the ball during their dribble? If they do, be ready to rule on the illegal advantage gained when the dribbler rocks back, then suddenly explodes past the closing defender who believes the ball handler picked up their dribble. Do they lift their pivot foot before starting their dribble? If so, the closely guarding defender will be looking to the official to penalize this illegal advantage.

And finally there is the fatigue factor to consider.

**Are you at your best for the game at hand, or are you bogged down mentally and physically from a heavy officiating schedule?**

The personal demands of work and family are a varied issue for every official, but the weariness created by working too many nights in a week for too many weeks can have a cumulative effect. Grinding through a heavy schedule may have officials cutting corners; maybe even looking at some games as "less important" than others, resulting in the official trying to conserve energy.

This is a pointed question that only the person looking back at you in the mirror can answer.

So, if an official wants to cut down on their number of missed plays in a game, they need to look to improve their on-court balance and positioning, as well as their pre-game player observations and the energy level they bring to each and every game.

The results will be pleasantly surprising.

# Going by the Book

I t would seem to be a fair statement to say that every official with at least a few games under their belt has experienced the chill of being waved to the table during a dead ball by the person handling the score book.

No matter what your experience level, there will be no reason to panic, if you understand the procedures for handling the two main reasons for being summoned to the table:

*Administrative Technical Fouls and Correctable Errors*

If you are beckoned to the table:

1) Calmly ask any coaches or other "helpers" gathered near the table to return to their respective benches.
2) Direct questions to the official scorer as to the accuracy of the home/official score book.
3) Request the head coaches come together to explain the problem and your ruling.
4) Don't be distracted by any explanation regarding why a player is not listed in the official book.

While administrative technical fouls have been greatly condensed to eliminate the parade of free throws for multiple bookkeeping mistakes, it is important to note the distinction between what happens in the pre-game **BEFORE and AFTER the 10-minute mark.**

A team's failure to provide its **roster and starting lineup** at least **10-minutes BEFORE the tip-off** results in **ONE administrative technical foul** being charged to the offending team.

**AFTER** the 10-minute mark, a team is charged with a maximum of **ONE technical foul** no matter how many times it changes a designated starter (except for illness, injury, illegal equipment, or to shoot a technical foul free throw) or any other roster change.

*NFHS Number Problems – It's in the C.A.R.D.S.*

Officials can use this acronym to help remember the book situations that would require issuing an administrative technical foul:

# **C**hanges **A**dditions **R**oster **D**uplications **S**tarters

- Changing the number of a player who is in the game or attempting to enter the game.
- Adding a name and number to the team member list.
- Failure to submit roster by 10-minute mark.
- Two players wearing duplicate numbers.
- Failure to submit starters by 10-minute mark.

Administrative technical fouls for **NFHS** are:
- Charged to the team.
- Count towards the team's bonus.
- **NOT** charged to the player or indirectly to the coach.

**NFHS Penalty: (Technical charged to Team A)**
- The game begins with Team B attempting two free-throws.
- Team B would inbound the ball at the division line.

You **would not** assess an administrative technical foul:
- If a player sitting on the bench is NOT LISTED in the official book <u>AND</u> there is NO ATTEMPT to enter the game by this player.
- Or if a player not listed in the book were to enter and leave the game before the error was discovered. The infraction must be penalized when it occurs.

*NCAA Number Problems – It's in the C.A.R.S.*

In NCAA Men's and Women's there is no administrative technical foul for duplicate numbers.

Administrative technical fouls for **NCAA Men** are:
- **NOT** charged to the team.

Administrative technical fouls - **NCAA Women** are:
- Charged to the team.
- Count towards the team's bonus.
- **NOT** charged to the player or indirectly to the coach.

## NCAA Men's & Women's Procedure:

- After shooting two free throws, the game would begin or resume at the Point of Interruption (opening game tipoff, or an in-game thrown in.)

Once the game has begun, any discrepancy between the listed starters and the actual starters **will not** result in any penalties. This infraction must be noticed before the ball becomes alive to start the game.

### *Correctable Errors (NFHS and NCAA)*

The other likely scenario requiring a trip to the table involves **Correctable Errors.** These are mistakes that **do not** involve errors in judgment or a rule interpretation.

There are five correctable error scenarios, and four of them pertain to problems with free throws (FT):

- Failure to award a merited free throw.
- Awarding an unmerited free throw.
- Permitting a wrong player to attempt a free throw.
- Attempting a free throw at the wrong basket.
- Mistakenly scoring or canceling a score.

In order to correct any of the above officials' mistakes, the errors must be recognized by an official no later than during the first dead ball after the clock has properly started.

*Correctable Error Timeline – Free Throws*

If the error is mistakenly counting or canceling a score while the clock is running, and the ball is dead, it must be recognized before the second live ball.

*Correctable Error Timeline – Field Goals*

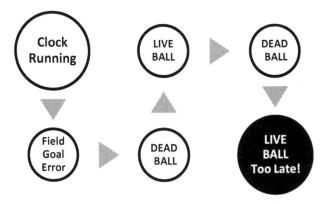

These timelines for correcting free throw and field goal errors (i.e. two point try vs. three point try mix-up), should not be confused with recordkeeping mistakes by the table, which can be fixed anytime they are discovered.

If the error is a FT by a wrong player or at the wrong basket or it is unmerited, all the activity **during the FT** is canceled (except unsporting, flagrant, intentional or technical fouls.)

Any points scored, fouls committed or time consumed prior to recognizing the correctable error will not be affected. It all shall stand as recorded.

If the error is corrected, play shall **resume from the point of interruption.**

However if you are awarding a merited FT and there has **been no change of possession since the error** was made, the play shall resume after the FT attempt(s).

Some preventative officiating during the pre-game can help sidestep many of the problems associated with administrative technical fouls, and a focused crew can almost always avoid correctable errors issues.

But if you do find yourself in one these predicaments, knowing how to correctly handle any administrative technical foul and correctable error situation will make for a stress-free stroll to the scorer's table in all of your future games.

*Rules Reference*
NFHS: 3-2-2b; 10-1-1-2a,b,c;  2-10-1:6
NCAA Men & Women: 3-3-1-3; 10-2-6; 10-2-8; 2-12-1:6

# Game Awareness

You may have been counseled as a child by a parent or teacher to always be aware of your surroundings as a great way to avoid trouble.

As a grown up basketball official this sage advice will serve you well on the court if you simply stay aware of the game events unfolding around you.

### *Bonus and Double Bonus Situations*

The scoreboard, as well as your mental calculator, should both keep you from getting bogged down in a correctable error scenario.

**If you are managing the game properly, you will remember to keep glancing up at the team fouls on the scoreboard.**

However if the scoreboard is malfunctioning, or you have a subpar clock operator, your internal radar tracking the approximate number of fouls called, should tell you to check if you are in, or close to being in, the bonus.

In the closing minutes of a game be aware if the team trailing is going to begin fouling to put their opponent at the foul line. Also, be aware if the team holding a lead near the end of the game has fouls to give before reaching the bonus, and they are choosing to commit non-shooting fouls.

Communicate **team control fouls** with clean signals and a clear voice so everyone will know there are no free throws to be shot.

**For NFHS & NCAA (Men & Women):** Team control (Team A) **does not end** when a defensive player (Team B) tips the ball away and it is loose on the floor. If a player on Team A were to commit a personal foul during the ensuing scramble to regain possession, this would be a team control foul and **no free throws are awarded**.

In NFHS there is **no** team control on a throw in.

In NCAA there **is** team control on a throw in.

### *A-P Arrow Situations*

Ideally, the person in charge of keeping the alternating possession arrow at the score table is thorough and competent, but ultimately, it is the officials' responsibility to know what team should be awarded possession on any jump ball scenario.

That means do whatever you need to do (a rubber band on your wrist, a whistle in your pocket) to get it right and avoid any problem. These props are somewhat frowned upon as you move up the officiating ladder, so you may need to wean yourself off at some point and rely strictly on your memory. But until then, use whatever discreet aid you find most comfortable.

> **Consider a quick gesture to a coach who you may make eye contact with at the end of each quarter (or half) to let them know whose ball it will be to resume play.**

## Substitute Situations

Observe which player(s) leave the game on each dead ball, because players may not return before the clock properly starts.

> **Remember, you can come IN and go OUT with the clock not starting, but you cannot go OUT and come IN, without the clock properly starting.**

## Clock Situations

Know how much time is on the game clock and shot clock on **EVERY** inbound scenario.

There is a subtle, almost indescribable, balance between being laser-focused on your officiating task at hand that allows you to block out the typical in-game catcalls and not be distracted, but still being able to observe, note and process almost everything that goes on in the gym.

> **Your officiating crew is the game manager of this particular contest and will need to be a part of any decision that will impact the playing of the game.**

So be sure to be aware of your game surroundings so you can preempt any problems, and rule on matters with all of the information necessary to get the situation right.

# Above the Ring Rulings

I t's been said that, *'patience is passion tamed,'* and when it comes to making decisions on plays above the ring, officials need to harness their enthusiasm and know what to look for while being in the best position to rule on the high-flying game action.

In a three-person crew, the Trail and the Center officials share the primary duties for "above the ring" rulings. In a two-person crew it is the Trail's primary responsibility to handle the plays at or on the ring.

Skill building for these lightning-rod rulings begins at the ground floor with footwork and positioning.

> **Officials should be in a "staggered" stance and have an "attack mode" frame of mind.**

The Trail and Center should be officiating off their **front foot** to stay on balance. This stance helps to heighten your awareness level which will keep surprises at a minimum, and have you focused on maintaining a clear vision of the ring.

Above the ring scenarios that will demand your patience and proficiency include:

- Basket Interference.
- Goaltending.
- Slapping the Backboard.
- Grasping the Basket.
- Blocked shots off the glass.
- Blocked shots on the glass.
- Ball passing over the backboard.

**Basket Interference** occurs when any player ...
- Touches the ball when the ball is on or within the basket.
- Touches the basket* when the ball is on or within the basket.
- Touches the ball when it's within the imaginary cylinder.
- Reaches up through the basket and touches the ball outside of the imaginary cylinder.
- Pulls down the ring, and before the ring returns to its original position, the ring touches the ball.

*The basket consists of the ring, flange, the braces and the net. The backboard is not part of the basket; therefore slapping the backboard cannot cause basket interference or goaltending.*

Basket Interference can occur on a try, a tap, a free throw and any time the ball is on or within the basket.

## Basket Interference Mechanics

When **offensive** Basket Interference occurs, the goal is disallowed and the ball is awarded to the opponent with a spot throw in closest to the violation. When **defensive** Basket Interference occurs, points are awarded and the opponent is given possession on the end line and is able to move along the end line.

For **Goaltending** to occur:
1. The try must be on its downward flight.*
2. The try must be outside the imaginary cylinder.
3. The try must have a chance to enter the basket.
4. The try must be above the basket's ring level.

*On a free throw, goaltending can occur on its upward or downward flight. This is also ruled a Technical Foul.

- For NCAA Men's goaltending on a free throw is a Class B technical and does not count towards the player or team foul total.
- For NCAA Women's and NFHS goaltending on a free throw does count towards the player and the team's foul total.

## Blocked Shots

For NCAA purposes, any try pinned above the basket's ring level is considered to be on its downward flight and therefore is considered goaltending.

Not so for NFHS. Any try pinned outside of the cylinder and on its upward flight is a legal defensive play.

## Slapping the Backboard and Over the Backboard

A player intentionally slapping or striking the backboard to distract a shooter or to vent frustration should be charged with a technical foul. The contacting of the backboard while the ball is in <u>or</u> is on the basket **is not** basket interference, by itself.

A player who slaps or strikes the backboard in a legitimate attempt to block a try for goal **should not** be penalized.

Any ball that passes over a rectangular backboard, should be ruled dead immediately and awarded to the team that did not cause the action. Play will resume with a spot throw-in closest to the violation.

**NFHS** - The ball would remain live if it were to pass over a fan shaped backboard.

Handling above the ring plays will be a critical part of your development and advancement as an official. If you have good balance, are patient and are focused on the key ingredients, your proficiency in this area will improve dramatically.

Finally, if you are in doubt, hold your whistle. More times than not, your patience will be rewarded with the correct ruling.

*Rules Reference*
*NFHS: 4-6; 4-22; 7-1-2b; 9-11; 9-12; 9-12 penalties*
*NCAA Men and Women: 4-5; 4-34; 7-1-3; 9-16; 9-17 penalties*
*NCAA Men: 10-6-1g*
*NCAA Women: 10-3-4*

# Leading From the Lead

The great American inventor Thomas Edison wisely stated that everything comes to him who hustles while he waits. For officials who find themselves working in the Lead position in a 3-person crew, they would do well to heed this sage advice in carrying out their duties on the end line.

Because of the Lead's close proximity to the goal, which is being attacked and defended with great vigor throughout each game, it is a position that can deliver a great deal of anxiety and therefore requires an equal amount of patience.

So in an effort to quell these anxious moments...

**Practice keeping your weight on your back foot in a staggered stance.**

This will help minimize the tendency to jump the gun and blow a quick whistle on a play that is still developing.

Just like a baseball player at the plate getting fooled with an off-speed pitch and lunging forward off balance, officials in the Lead position will be aided in their goal to remain patient by keeping their weight on their back foot.

This patient, **call what you see - see what you call** approach strengthens your resolve not to guess on plays and to rely more on the aggressive mindset of your partners in the Trail and Center positions.

Now because the game of basketball has shifted from the traditional style of pounding the ball into the post, to a game of players slashing hard to the rim for a layup or to kick the ball out to a wide open jump shooter when met with resistance, the Lead must work to identify the secondary defenders who are moving over to stop the penetrating dribbler.

> **The Lead should focus on the defenders coming to help their beaten teammate to determine if they have established a legal guarding position, should contact with the dribbler/airborne shooter occur.**

In **NFHS and NCAA**, the lane is typically a split area of responsibility for both the Center and Lead.

However, many times the Center cannot see the secondary defender, so the Lead must understand they are to officiate this play and not feel as if they are reaching out of their primary area.

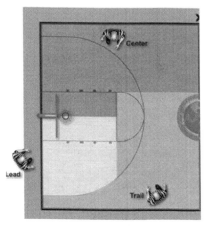

*Diagram showing the Lead official in the "Closed Down" position in a good location to rule on plays in their primary coverage area and assist the Center with secondary defenders.*

With the Lead's patient approach, officials will begin to consistently reward good blocks with no whistles, and leave the Center to aggressively penalize fouls from behind.

While the Lead is mainly responsible for dictating rotations to ensure the best court coverage, it is important for the Lead to understand when to close down (also called "pinching the paint") and when to move briskly to the other side. For instance, the Lead will close down on an immediate drive to the basket in order to get the best angle to see the play develop.

**The official transitioning from the Trail to the new Lead should most times hustle to the "closed down spot" on the end line and move to mirror the ball as the offensive team comes into the front court.**

Knowing the location of the ball is more of a "feel" with your peripheral vision than tracking it with your eyes. You need to practice officiating with a "big picture" mentality and not locked into a tunnel vision mindset. Take a quick peek at the point guard's eyes; they will tip you to where the play is going to develop.

Now find the key players in your area. This will help you to know when you will rotate.

While looking for opportunities to rotate, it may be more helpful to offer a few practical guidelines on when the Lead **WOULD NOT** want to rotate.

The Lead will wait on drives to the basket; on a try or tap for goal, and when the ball is below the foul line and being passed cross court.

In these instances, the Lead will hold their ground and work patiently to get the best open angle.

If you have begun to rotate when one of these situations occurs, **it is best to go back** to your original spot.

**Immediate Pass**

**Immediate Try for Goal**

**Immediate Dribble Drive to the Basket**

**The '3' Immediates**

= <u>NO</u> ROTATION

When you do rotate in the Lead position, develop a habit of glancing at the shot clock and game clock. This will give you a great starting point should a problem occur in the interim. And also glance back over your shoulder to make sure you're not missing anything behind you.

And with a "big picture" mentality, the Lead will act like a free safety in football and see how the offense is setting up where the ball is likely going and what the defensive team will attempt to stop.

Keep in mind the Lead is responsible for post play and strong side rebounding (the side of the court where the ball is) so take a position deep enough on the end line to get the best angle to officiate the plays in this area.

As the pace of the game quickens, it is critical to remember that on fast-breaks, the new Lead must be aware of the offensive player pulling up to attempt a three-point shot.

Also the Lead has to assist with press coverage and should take a position near the division line, when all of the players are in the backcourt, but without letting any player get behind them.

If the play is spread out, the Lead could start at the free throw line extended and work up to the division line.

Finally, with an emphasis on allowing freedom of movement, it's important to keep the lane area from becoming clogged with players.

When the ball is **ABOVE** the free throw line extended, it is the Lead's responsibility to call three-second violations. This is not a "game interrupter" call, but rather a clear and consistent ruling that will promote a good flow to the game and reduce rough interior play.

So adhering to the enlightened advice of, 'hustling while you wait' and embracing these guidelines for officiating in the Lead, will have your officiating skills and the games you work shining as bright as any incandescent bulb!

# On The Trail and in the Center

The counter-balance to the recommended patient approach to working in the Lead position is an aggressive "attack mode" mentality suggested for handling your duties in the Trail and Center spots.

This complementary strategy is designed to provide seamless court coverage and build a level of comfort in your officiating crew with a balanced temperament coming from each position.

**An "attack mode" approach in the Trail and Center positions means your weight is now on your front foot farthest from the basket in a staggered stance and you are bringing a more aggressive mindset to these spots by keeping your feet active.**

In the Trail and Center you must let your feet follow your eyes. Stay active – get on the floor if you have to -- and constantly work for the best angle to see through the competitive matchups you are monitoring. The Trail and Center slots are not positions to idle in "park" or neutral. These spots demand near-constant shifting of your feet to find a clear view of the action and to be leaning forward with a poised readiness to manage the fast-paced activity in front of you.

You are moving with purpose and not burning energy with wasted hustle that makes you appear to be scrambling to keep up with the play, you need to understand how to react to the player activity in your area.

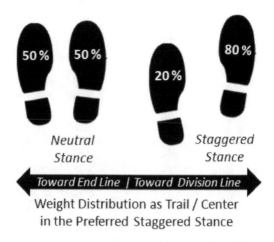

Neutral
Stance

Staggered
Stance

◀ Toward End Line | Toward Division Line ▶

Weight Distribution as Trail / Center
in the Preferred Staggered Stance

When a dribbler is coming at you, you are going to **move opposite of the flow so you can get on top of the play.** Now there is the potential to be caught in the cross-fire if there is a quick steal, but this is where the "on your toes" attack mode mentality will keep you better prepared to dodge the change of direction action.

There is a school of thought on diving down on drives to the basket, and no doubt this strategy will serve the Center well on getting a better look at a player coming along the end line from the strong side for a reverse layup, or a jump shooter who is front of you, but more often than not, getting on top of the play with a sort of "mini-Trail" approach will allow you to officiate more players with a greater court vision.

Think of the Center position as a "glider" or "cleaner" position…In this spot you will glide confidently from foul line to foul line and will be cleaning up off-the-ball activity such as holding, block-charges, illegal screens, and rerouting or bumping any cutting players.

When the ball is in the front court, the Center is responsible for curling plays (or spin moves to the basket by the low post player.) Also, the Center is responsible for crossing plays. That is to say, a dribbler coming from the Trail and Lead's side and crossing into the Center's area of coverage. When the dribbler slashes to the basket, your best angle to stay connected to the play will likely be on the top side of the play.

In the Center slot you want to practice letting the play clear in front of you. Don't just turn and shuffle up court too early assuming a change of possession rebound will ensue on the missed field goal attempt. A hasty departure by the Center will leave the Lead/new Trail to officiate any contested weak-side rebound activity or backcourt pressure applied by the new defensive team.

On the subject of rebounding activity, keep in mind the Center has weak-side responsibility (the Lead has strong-side responsibility) and the Trail position oversees all rebounding responsibilities.

In all post play activity, the Trail and the Center should focus on all foot movement, and the **Lead** should concentrate on everything **above the player's waist.**

The Trail also is responsible for maintaining all freedom of movement coming across the division line and above the foul line when the offensive team settles in the front court. This requires a clear understanding and consistent enforcement of defensive contact that restricts the dribbler's movement or other impediments to the offensive flow of the game.

Any contact by the defender's hand or body that impedes or reroutes the offensive player's movement is a foul and must be called.

With the defender's hands, there is an important difference between "hot stove" touching and "tactile" touching.

Hot stove contact is quick, repeated hand taps by the defender that have a cumulative effect of annoying and disrupting the offensive player's rhythm and concentration. Once this pattern is observed, it should be ruled a foul. If left to continue, the offensive player will take matters into their own hands and will slap away or push off the defender.

However, tactile touching by the defender is incidental contact and should not be ruled a foul. In this instance the defender is using an isolated non-disruptive gesture to "feel" where the offensive player is.

Know this critical difference between incidental and illegal contact.

Although not specifically noted as an approved NCAA or NFHS signal, many officials voice additional information when reporting the foul to the table.

Such examples are …

> *"Blue..21…Reroute!* *"Blue..21…Stayed Hand!*
> *"Blue..21…Two Hands!*

This will emphatically tell the player and coach the specifics of the infraction.

Keep in mind, the Trail will officiate what the Lead cannot; meaning the pesky secondary defender or the player coming to double team.

> **The Trail and the Center should always protect the Lead's backside and handle the potential defender and rebounder from behind.**

Conversely, the Lead will always protect the Trail and the Center's front side.

Finally, there is no 'magic spot' on the floor that will always give you the best angle. Whether it is the Trail or the Center positions, the main objective is to get the best open angle on the play and that will always require active feet and plenty of movement.

So develop a clear understanding of the areas of responsibility and keep an even-handed approach to enforcing the tips offered in these two chapters dealing with the Lead, Center and Trail positions and you will come a long way to dramatically improving your game management skills.

# SDF: Start – Develop – Finish

The trio of words used to name this topic is meant to help officials correctly and consistently rule on situations involving offensive players with the ball on a path to the basket.

When a player driving to the basket is bumped or slightly rerouted by a defender without losing control of the ball, the official needs a patient whistle to let the offensive player get into the act of shooting.

**Officials need to be conscious of the fact that a quick whistle in this scenario would actually penalize the offensive player/team.**

Quick whistles often hinder an offensive team's opportunity to score a goal. A hasty whistle may result in a throw-in (which could easily lead to a turnover) or a bonus free throw situation, instead of a goal, or a three-point play opportunity.

To be clear, the "SDF" philosophy is not advocating officials pass on fouls, but merely suggests for plays **below the free throw line extended** that officials take a "big picture" mentality and consider who is being penalized on a quick whistle for contact that occurs as the offensive player is on a path to the basket.

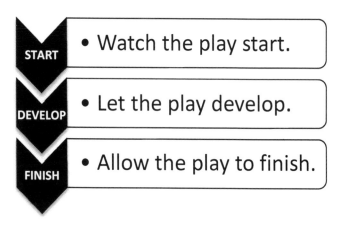

**START** • Watch the play start.

**DEVELOP** • Let the play develop.

**FINISH** • Allow the play to finish.

Integrate the "**START – DEVELOP – FINISH**" mindset with your approach to continuous motion, and you will have a more consistent delivery for ruling on contact by defenders on players driving to the basket.

# Shot Blocking --- What To Look For

**N**othing seems to evoke more fury from players, coaches and spectators then when an official calls a foul on what half of the gym feels is a good, clean block of a field goal attempt.

Knowing what to look for and where an official should focus their attention during a blocked shot attempt will greatly reduce those 'spotlight moments' and allow the game to maintain its great flow. A good no-call might even kick-start a rhythm in a game that up to this point had been somewhat disjointed.

Consider the concept that if a defender blocks the shot, then has body contact, there is no foul.

With the notable exception of high-speed action on a breakaway attempt where the contact may come after the block, but the airborne offensive player is in such a vulnerable position, the contact should be ruled a foul.

However, if the game action sequence is body contact, then the blocked shot, you likely have a defensive foul on the play.

Now for contested plays under and around the basket, officials must be more aware of the **Principle of Verticality**. Allowing a defensive player to jump **straight up** and maintain a legal guarding position and therefore not be penalized with a foul for contact caused by an offensive player breaking the defender's plane.

**The Principle of Verticality is less of a factor when evaluating plays on the perimeter as compared to plays in the post area.**

For plays in the open court, it is critical for officials to watch the shooter and defender rise in the air and return to the floor.

Officials need to guard against being over-anxious to signal on three-point shot attempts because the focus tends to then follow the ball and not stay with the shooter.

There is plenty of time to adequately signal if the shot being attempted is behind the three-point arc, so don't rush.

# Observing Blocked Shots –
## Key Points to Consider

1) Find the defender's guard hand.

2) If the defender's hand is **above or equal** to the height of the ball, hand contact by the defender is likely on the ball. This results in a good clean block.

3) If the defender's hand is **below** the height of the ball, hand contact by the defender is likely on the shooter's wrist or arm. This should be ruled a foul.

On a 'bang-bang' play where the ball pops up or goes straight up, most likely a foul has occurred. This is caused by the defender's hand contact with the offensive player's forearm.

Logically, if the ball suddenly dives straight down it is likely the result of the defender's hand contact directly on the ball. Therefore, this play is a legal strip or block and no reason for an official to rule it a foul.

A consistent application of this approach to monitoring blocks or strips, will in the long run, be appreciated by everyone involved with the game you are working.

# Fouls on Rebounds

**P**revious chapters have stressed the importance of having a 'patient whistle' to ensure officials see the entire play and not to rule too early and cause a disruption in the flow of the game  and saddle players with needless fouls.

This patient approach is vital when evaluating player contact during all rebound activity.

**A "possession consequence" mindset** is a very effective way to determine if the player contact should be ruled a foul and will reinforce the value of a patient whistle.

Simply stated, if there is player contact that **does not** result in a change of possession and **does not** have any negative consequence (i.e. cause the opponent to commit a violation), then hold your whistle and let the play continue.

However, if there is player contact that **does** result in a change of possession or **does** have a negative consequence (i.e. unfairly reduces the opponent's chances of securing the rebound), then blow your whistle after patiently viewing the entire play.

An equal part of diligence must accompany an official's patient approach in cleaning up all contact that is excessive and will most certainly lead to rough physical play. This type of non-basketball contact requires a quick whistle to clearly demonstrate that under no circumstances will it be tolerated.

To return the spotlight back to the normal body contact involved in players actively competing to secure possession of the ball on rebounds, it seems the study of game tape will bear out that it is the secondary rebounder coming out of nowhere that commits much of the illegal contact.

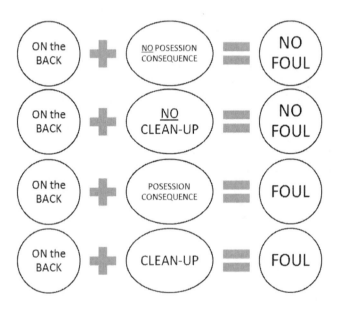

*Diagram: Using the Possession Consequence mindset when dealing with "on the back" situations can help an official understand when a foul should be ruled.*

Using this premise, it is important for the Trail to concentrate on the players above the foul line who often get a running head start and leap deep into the lane to dislodge an opponent from behind.

> **It is the Trail and Center's responsibility to protect the Lead's weak side and officiate the plays on the Lead's back side that are not as visible to them.**

Both the Trail and Center must be in an **attack mode stance** and be ready for the fast-paced game action, or they will often miss a foul or violation.

A patient approach with a big picture view will keep officials from unfairly calling a foul on a player simply because that player is a better leaper than the opponent in front of them.

Contact **ON** a player's back that dislodges them from their spot on the floor, or where they jumped from, **IS** a foul and should be called.

> **Incidental contact from a player as they leap OVER and above an opponent to secure a rebound IS NOT necessarily a foul.**

This is a situation that when ruled on correctly demonstrates maturity and meaningful growth in an official's development and will grab the attention of any astute observer.

# RSBQ

The title of this chapter is not a hip way of asking you to reply to a cookout invitation, but rather a helpful acronym to assist in your judgment of evaluating contact by a defensive player on the perimeter or on moves to the basket.

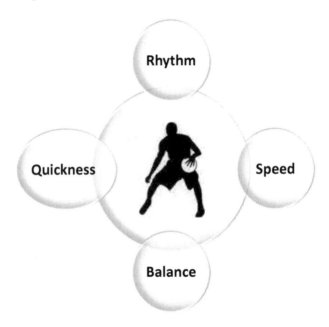

That is to say, you are to monitor the **R**hythm, **S**peed, **B**alance and **Q**uickness of the offensive players in your area.

> If <u>any</u> of these four items are affected by a defensive player, it should be ruled a foul, provided a scoring opportunity does not exist.

This RSBQ method may offer a more complete picture for officials and prove to be a better guideline for evaluating contact on the perimeter or on drives to the goal, than the respected 'advantage-disadvantage' philosophy.

A patient whistle will consistently serve you well by allowing the play to develop and not, in effect, penalize the offensive team by blowing a quick whistle.

An offensive player in the backcourt or on the frontcourt perimeter who has their "RSBQ" impeded, a foul should be called on the defender.

However, on plays where the offensive player with the ball has beaten their defender despite having their "RSBQ" altered slightly, and has created a scoring opportunity or a defensive mismatch for a potential easy basket, the official should exercise restraint and allow the play to continue.

> **Perhaps the only thing worse than a premature whistle that takes away an easy basket and "rewards" the offensive team with an inbounds throw-in, is the official who blew their whistle being oblivious to the situation they just created.**

The old axiom about people who *"don't know what they don't know"* being the most dangerous, holds true for officials as well. If you are unaware that your early whistle has in effect penalized the offensive team by denying them an opportunity for a field goal and/or free throw attempt(s), then there is no chance to correct your mistake. It will likely happen again with a potentially negative cumulative effect.

Keep in mind there is a critical difference between calling a ticky-tack "and one" foul, and contact that affects "RSBQ" and should be penalized with a foul.

You do not want to deny an offensive player a legitimate three-point opportunity for contact that goes beyond being marginal or incidental (i.e. any blow or contact to the head) or affecting a player's balance and their ability to protect themselves returning to the floor.

Be conscious of monitoring an offensive player's **rhythm, speed, balance and quickness** being disrupted on the perimeter, as well as offering a patient whistle on defensive contact where the offensive player has a potential scoring opportunity; and you will no doubt be asked to RSVP to many more quality basketball assignments from your supervisor!

# Match Ups

**I**n officiating clinics and classroom instruction on the subject of court coverage, much of the discussion centers around the primary areas of responsibility.

And while there is no doubt an official need a solid understanding of the boundaries for two and three person officiating crews, it is suggested that you drill down further in your area of coverage and focus on the **player matchups** within your area.

The **matchup concept** can be broken down into three categories:

A **competitive matchup** in your area of coverage has two players in close proximity to each other who may be coming together to compete as the offensive team attempts to run a play.

This could result in a defender trying to ward off a screen being set against them, or having to defend a play taking shape that will attempt to score in their defensive area.

**Officials need to monitor the players in their primary area with an understanding of what may be coming based on prior game action.**

Officials cannot referee in a vacuum. If a particular player matchup has been favorable to one team, you can assume that team will look to continue to exploit the advantage until their opponent makes an adjustment to try to eliminate the defensive shortcoming.

Monitor these competitive matchups from the outset to have the complete picture when this escalates into an active matchup.

An **active matchup** is a play where a defender is closely guarding a player with the ball as they are looking to execute a play that will create an advantageous situation leading to a scoring attempt.

These active matchups can occur between two post players or with two players isolated on the perimeter. There will likely be some body contact as the defender attempts to gird themselves for the offensive player's best move.

It is the official's responsibility to see the entire play develop to be able to correctly determine if the defender has established legal guarding position, or if any of the hand/body contact has garnered an illegal advantage for the defender.

If either player feels their opponent is being overly aggressive, this scenario could get dialed up to an **engaged matchup** which will need your immediate attention.

An **engaged matchup** is one that exhibits verbal and/or physical intimidation by one or both players and has he serious potential to escalate into conduct that will warrant personal and/or technical fouls.

**If you have been properly officiating the matchups in your area, then quite often you will be able to diffuse this situation before any punitive measures need to be administered.**

A calm but stern warning to both players as you move up the floor, or ideally during a dead ball, can often allow the players to save face and end their jousting.

Also, notify your partners (either verbally or with eye contact and a simple hand gesture) of your engaged matchup so a collective effort can be made to monitor from all angles this potentially volatile situation.

Investing your time wisely during pre-game warm ups can also greatly assist you with officiating your matchups.

Identify the possible post players for each team and try to gauge if there is going to be any clear mismatch issues one team might attempt to exploit.

Make a mental note of the players who stand out on the team:

- The "go to" star player.
- The less skilled, muscled up enforcer.
- The quick, slashing player.

These players will likely command much of your attention when they are in the game.

As the game progresses you may want to ask yourself these questions when the horn sounds for a substitution:

- Why is this player coming into the game?
- Are they coming in to shoot the "three?"
- Are they coming in to play defense and try to cool off a hot scorer?
- Are they coming in to act as an enforcer to intimidate or distract a key opponent?

Sharpen your focus to deal with the matchups in your area, as opposed to simply monitoring the boundaries of your primary area, and you will contribute greatly to the overall success of your game.

# WIF -- Windup, Impact and Follow Through

The acronym "WIF" stands for **W**indup, **I**mpact and **F**ollow Through and is designed to help officials judge if the contact delivered to an offensive player should be ruled an intentional or flagrant foul.

**Quite simply, if two of the three "WIF" elements take place in the play you are monitoring, then you should likely rule an intentional foul.**

For the incident to be judged a flagrant foul, you will need to quickly but thoroughly process the severity of the contact and the resulting effects of it.

Keep in mind, flagrant fouls rarely happen in a vacuum. There is normally some preceding on-court drama that is the catalyst for the overly aggressive contact. Doing a good job of monitoring the temperature of your game can go a long way to diffusing potentially volatile situations and pre-empting any physical confrontations between players.

However, if there is a hard foul given in your game, quickly move to the 'victim' and not the player delivering the contact. The recipient of the foul is likely going to be angry and may feel they must defend themselves and step to the perpetrator.

In most cases, the player who is fouled does not want to fight, so an official's swift intervention will allow the player to save face.

An empathic tone of voice with the player will many times quell the situation immediately. If the officials demonstrate they will firmly deal with overly aggressive rough play, then the players will usually not feel compelled to take matters into their own hands.

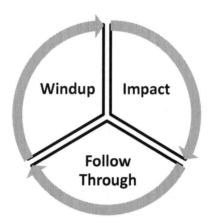

It is when players believe they must mete out their own justice and they cannot rely on the officials to keep order that overly aggressive contact and subsequent retaliation occurs.

To that end, don't be afraid to quietly compliment a player for showing restraint after being on the receiving end of a hard foul. A short, simple and non-partisan acknowledgement of a player's good judgment may have some long-lasting effects with that player, as well as others.

*When is an intentional foul,*
***NOT*** *an intentional foul?*

The answer is when the defensive team makes a half-hearted attempt to play the ball, but clearly is intending to foul in order to stop the clock in the closing minutes of a game. The trailing team needs to get their opponent into the bonus and onto the foul line where they will have the opportunity to rebound a missed free throw and possibly narrow the score.

Now meaningful debates have raged between those officials who take a literal interpretation on this scenario and claim a "foul is a foul," and those with a more liberal view to ruling on such contact.

**In going beyond the rules, it might be advisable to exercise restraint when it comes to doling out intentional fouls in the final moments of a game.**

These foul rulings may result in officials having to penalize exasperated coaches with technical fouls because the other team is receiving two shots and the ball, instead of the ball for an inbound throw-in or bonus free throw attempts.

The officials accomplished goal of remaining nearly invisible to the players, coaches and spectators for most of the game has now been thwarted by their literal interpretation of what is an intentional foul and has placed the spotlight clearly on them.

Knowing to look for a **"WIF" – Wind Up, Impact and Follow Through** – to determine if the player contact should be ruled intentional or flagrant, and how to best interpret contact in the closing minutes of a game will serve both the officials and the game well, in the long run.

# Hand Checks

In an effort to help draw a clearer picture of what defensive hand contact should actually be ruled a hand checking foul, officials can use these offerings to help consistently distinguish between the subtle variations of this pesky defensive pressure.

**A defender using their hands or arms to reroute or impede an offensive player's movement is guilty of hand checking, and this conduct must be ruled a foul.**

This illegal contact can be delivered in several ways:

**Stayed hands -** when a defender places their hand (or hands) on some part of an offensive player and keeps it there as a measure of some control.

**Stayed hands** is a foul and it must be called.

The same is true of a **defensive forearm** placed on an offensive player to offer some level of physical resistance by the defender. This is a foul and it must be called consistently.

Constant touching of a dribbler by a defender as they make their way up or across the floor is a **"hot stove"** tactic and this action is a foul.

These are not "game interrupter" fouls. The defender's repeated hand strikes to the offensive player's body will have a cumulative effect of rerouting or impeding the dribbler to slow or change their direction and allow the beaten defensive player time to regroup and regain their position on the dribbler.

> **A defender making hand contact to the body of the player they are guarding to merely feel where they are as they look off the ball, or for the ball, are "tactile touches" and this contact should not be considered a foul.**

A tactile touch is contact that **does not** impede or reroute an offensive player, but rather is contact meant to help the defender gauge where the player they are guarding is. This is hand contact by the defender without applying physical pressure to the offensive player.

If you call a tactile touch a hand checking foul, you will undoubtedly be **setting the bar too low** on what a foul is and creating a standard that will be extremely difficult for you and your partners to consistently enforce.

However, when a benign touch becomes repetitive and more forceful, this is a **"hot stove"** situation that is putting the offensive player at an illegal disadvantage and must be ruled a foul.

It is important to note, this is for contact above the free throw line extended.

When the dribbler is on a path to the basket below the foul line, take a more patient approach. Let the play **START**, **DEVELOP** and **FINISH** to avoid calling a foul too soon and ultimately penalize the offensive player.

The pre-game warm up will provide another excellent opportunity to wisely invest your time and observe the players as they perform their defensive drills. Look for the players who instinctively play defense with their hands and make a mental note of it.

> **An official may even want to discreetly mention to a player to be careful with their hand-checking tactics.**

Simply deliver an even-toned comment as a cautionary word of advice, and move on.

While not officially in the mechanics guide, many veteran officials try to incorporate words like, "reroute" or "impeding the progress" when offering a brief explanation to a coach on what their defender did wrong.

Painting clear pictures for distinguishing what is and is not a hand checking foul, and offering this insight to coaches in concise sound bites, will no doubt improve your game and your stature among coaches and assignors.

# Body Language & Signals

I t is often said that communication consists of 93% body language and physical cues.

If this percentage is remotely accurately, it greatly underscores the importance of how officials present themselves before, during and after a basketball game.

Now it's not acceptable for an official to don a pair of sunglasses like many of the participants wear in high-stakes card games, but...

### Officials need to develop their own poker face.

Not a scowl or any type of look that portrays an off-putting arrogance or swagger, but rather more of a non-threatening all-business demeanor that conveys both a sense of fairness and firmness about you.

The very best officials are those with an on-court presence that serve to diffuse volatile situations, not ignite them further. Be the official who can absorb the initial outburst of a coach or player without taking it personal, while having an inner-sensor that knows when the line of decorum has been crossed and the conduct must be dispassionately dealt with.

It seems all officials know exactly how to handle confrontational situations in the games they watch in person or on TV. Calmly and confidently officials explain how they would handle the tense moment they are observing.

So the challenge is to be able to channel this cool persona when you find the temperature rising in one of your own games. To work on being able to call on that "out-of-body" crisis management expertise that comes so easily in games you're watching.

This confident demeanor starts with a thorough knowledge of the rules.

The authors of the popular website, **"60 Seconds on Officiating,"** (www.ref60.com) proclaim that...

## 'Rule competency breeds calmness and confidence in chaos.'

There is no doubt an official can weather criticism better when they know they are absolutely correct in their interpretation of a rule.

On the contrary, it can be a difficult task to confidently administer a ruling when thoughts of doubt are filling your mind.

So, as you work on your official body language makeover, remember to be conscious of:

## Your Facial Expression

Develop you own poker face that shows ideally no emotion. Don't let your expression give the impression you are bored, or tired, or nervous, or angry.

If sarcasm is part of your repertoire, leave it in the parking lot. There is no place for rolling your eyes or laughing derisively at a comment or gesture made by a coach, player or spectator.

## Your Posture

When observing the players during warm ups, try to use a military parade rest stance. Keep your hands out of your pants and jacket pockets, and off of your hips.

## Your Attitude

Show energy, but be mindful of showboating. The fans paid to see the players perform, not you.

While laughing with your partner, a coach or a spectator may seem harmless, keep in mind a player or team struggling in a particular game, or possibly having a challenging season, will likely not see the humor in what is amusing you.

**Practice being the best official you can be, and bring that 'package' to every game you work.**

Don't be damned with the reputation as an official who only works hard in the "big games" or when a supervisor or assignor is in the building.

Crisp, clean signals go hand-in-hand with demonstrating good body language.
Show energy with good hand signals; with an emphasis on being specific and clear. Practice exuding confidence, but not arrogance. Your precision and hustle will speak louder about your attitude than anything you might say on your behalf.

Work on developing your cadence:

- Hustle to your spot of the floor in clear vision of the table.
- Verbally give the jersey color of the offending team.
- Verbally and with clear hand signals give the number of the offending player.
- Verbally and with clear hand signals indicate the number of shots or location of the throw in.

Lastly, find the duality of your inner-voice.

> **Your normal voice is for obvious fouls and violations. Your command voice is for tense game moments that fairly but firmly leave no doubt you are in charge.**

At the end of the day, if the extremely high percentage of non-verbal communications is accurate, then what you do and how you act on the court will be much more impactful than whatever you could possibly say.

# Variation of Whistles

**I**t doesn't seem to take officials very long to recognize they have the ability to speak with, and through, their whistles.

A sharp, crisp and **IMMEDIATE** whistle will send a clear authoritative message that certain conduct will be ruled on without hesitation.

> **Hand-checking on the perimeter, bumping the cutter coming through the lane, or an aggressive on-the back rebounding foul, are all non-basketball plays. These can lead to rough play and need to be called immediately.**

A **DOUBLE-TOOT** on your whistle will quickly let your partners know you have something different (a walk before the foul; a foul on the floor before the shot) that occurred a split-second earlier and will preempt their call.

However, a **DOUBLE WHISTLE**, where two (or more) officials sound their whistles on the same play, can produce instant trouble if the officials offer differing preliminary signals.

A thorough pre-game review of your **double whistle procedure** will greatly reduce the chances of this problem arising in one of your games.

## Double Whistle Checklist

- Step into your partner's visual field.
- Make good eye contact with the other calling official.
- Move towards the play.
- Offer a verbal acknowledgement. (i.e. "I have it!" or "You take it!")
- Now give a preliminary signal.
- Other official should drop their stopped clock signal. (closed fist or open hand)

**If you have several double whistles, you may want to consider sharing the load.**

Make eye contact along with a short verbal directive ("take it" or "you got it.") so one official is not calling all of the fouls. This distribution of the double whistle work load will help your partner develop their rhythm and give them credibility with coaches, players and fans that may pay huge dividends in the closing minutes of a tight game.

Another pesky play that can lead to double whistle scenarios is a **BLOCK-CHARGE** crash in the lane.

It is advisable to consider the following in a 3-person crew:

- Defer to the Lead if they are in a closed down position as they have the best vantage point.
- Allow the Trail and Center to follow any kick-out pass to the wing or corners and stay with this play.
- On contact in the lane that started as a drive to the basket from the Center's matchup area, the Lead should yield to the Center's whistle.

*(Continued)*

---

**74**

- All officials should be cognizant of illegal block/charge contact in the lane, and not freeze up on the whistle, because of uncertainty about whose area is primary.
- Bottom line, make sure to enforce the obvious fouls, regardless of who was "supposed" to blow the whistle.

Note: In a two-person crew, the lead official typically takes ALL plays coming toward them in the lane.

**Keep a PATIENT WHISTLE as the Lead official, especially while monitoring drives toward the basket.**

Remember, let the plays below the foul line develop and finish. This minimizes the official prematurely stopping the game and penalizing the offensive team. Quick whistles may deny a scoring attempt which results in resuming play with an inbounds throw in.

The same "patient whistle" practice would apply for rebounding scenarios. If the contact is not severe and there is no loss of possession (or defensive advantage) caused by incidental contact, then it is advisable to hold your whistle and allow the play to continue.

You will find the more your whistle is used as an effective communication tool, the less talking you will ultimately have to do.

# Preparing for the Final Moments

A clay pot sitting in the sun will always be a clay pot until it goes through the white heat of the furnace to become porcelain.

The noted philosopher credited with this remark about dealing with adversity was not referring to basketball officials, but the analogy still applies.

**At times, the final minutes of a fiercely contested game, in a jam-packed gym, can feel hotter than any cauldron.**

The following are some cool, soothing tips to mentally call on to keep you and your partner(s) out of the fire as the game heats up.

*Timeouts-*
*For more than just catching your breath!*

- Last things first: remember which team will inbound the ball, and where. If it's an end-line throw-in, can the player run, or is it a spot throw-in?
- Use this break in the action to quickly discuss with your partner(s) any coverage issues and to consider where the offensive team may try to attack.

*(Continued)*

- Head off any late substitutions hiccups, with a "first horn" warning that includes the phrase, *"no more substitutions."*
- Do not inbound the ball without making sure you have 10 players set, and partner(s) ready to resume play.

## *Play the Game*

Granted, you are there to officiate what transpires in the game and this is not a scripted performance, but do not officiate the contest in a vacuum. Stay mentally into the possible strategies of both teams.

If a team needs to foul in order to get close to or into the bonus, give them what they want.

**Contact that perhaps wasn't a foul up to this point, <u>now</u> should be strongly considered to be ruled a foul, if that is the defensive team's intention.**

Some officials may take exception to this statement and argue a literal interpretation of, *'if it wasn't a foul in the first minute, it isn't a foul in the last minute.'* However sticking with this position will increase the chances of you having to quickly determine if the subsequent escalated contact should be ruled intentional, and create a scenario that could very likely have been avoided.

To that end, be alert for an aggressive foul. When the hard foul occurs, blow your whistle, signal to stop the clock and quickly replay the scenario in your mind, then confidently decide if you are going to rule this an intentional foul.

Also, anticipate a timeout request if the player with the ball gets trapped, or is unable to complete a throw-in, or after a made basket by either team. The 'off' official should attempt to steal a glance in the direction of the bench, especially if the noise level is high.

## *Throw-Ins – What happened?*

Be alert for an anxious defense that may reach through the plane. Be prepared to rule if the player:

- Breaks the plane – a warning.
- Touches the ball – a technical foul.
- Touches the player – an intentional foul.

    However, if the player inbounding breaks the plane with the ball, the defender may slap the ball away or may grab it resulting in a jump ball.

- Disqualifications – avoid conflict.

There will no doubt be some attrition of players in a hard-fought contest, so if you call the fifth foul on a player, let your partner handle the notification of the player and coach.

First, notify the coach, then the disqualified player.

**Finally, no timeout is to be granted until the substitution for the disqualified player is made.**

Just as a team's field goals, free throws and turnovers are more magnified in the closing minutes of a close game; so too are an official's rulings.

If you are mindful of these tips, you will no doubt come through the fire a more polished, and a more highly regarded official.

# What's Your Officiating Personality?

**M**uch has been studied and written over the years regarding various personality types of individuals and how these behavioral tendencies interact together.

Why is this important?

Your personality "defines" you professionally – and brands you during the developmental years.

Which of the following qualities describes YOU as an official?

*Qualities of an Open Officiating Personality*

- People Oriented.
- Friendly, adaptable, action-oriented.
- Tend to be doers who are focused on immediate results.
- Usually warm-hearted with visible passion and love for the game.
- Extremely approachable by anyone. Will answer questions asked in a professional manner, given the circumstances.
- Doesn't mind being the crew chief or handling problems on the court.

- Tends to be more quiet and reflective.
- Logical mind that many times will be in-flexible and non-wavering.
- Does not like conflict.
- Stable and practical but not particularly inventive.
- Perceptive of other's feelings but often will not react or change their mind based on a current situation.
- Tends to ignore conflict or difficult questions from colleagues or coaches.
- Un-approachable by peers or antagonists.
- Escalates issues and easily can be engaged in arguments with coaches.

## PERSONALITY

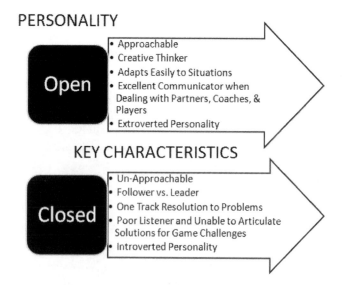

**Open**
- Approachable
- Creative Thinker
- Adapts Easily to Situations
- Excellent Communicator when Dealing with Partners, Coaches, & Players
- Extroverted Personality

## KEY CHARACTERISTICS

**Closed**
- Un-Approachable
- Follower vs. Leader
- One Track Resolution to Problems
- Poor Listener and Unable to Articulate Solutions for Game Challenges
- Introverted Personality

Being human, we all have different personalities. Knowing your personality make-up and that of the crew and coaches can help make difficult situations easier to handle.

# Personalities and Officiating Experience

**A**s previously discussed, personalities define us as officials throughout our career. Many young referees are tagged as hard to deal with, un-approachable and thick headed. Others gain the reputation of being easy to work with, very personable, while still being quite professional.

If you take the officiating personality (Open vs. Closed) and overlay experience, you have the potential for a great mixture or a volatile combination.

Here are four combinations of personality and experience. Which one of these "hybrid" types are YOU?

## *Type A:*
### *Experts / Veterans with Open Personalities*

These officials are the most desirable to work with from a partner (or coaching) perspective. This is a person that has learned their craft, is quite knowledgeable but still maintains an "open" attitude toward other people.

These officials are extremely approachable and have great inter-professional relationships with their colleagues. Typically preferred, these referees usually have a great working rapport with their supervisors / assignors and are usually requested by coaches of similar personality type.

## Type B:
### Novices with Open Personalities

Second only to more experienced officials (Type A), these up and coming referees have the correct mindset to be successful in this extremely competitive environment.

During the professional growth period, a Type B official asks many questions of their peers and is quite willing to take constructive criticism to foster learning.

**Coaches of a similar personality type will tolerate mistakes made by these referees as they understand the learning curve can be quite steep in this game.**

Being of open personality, they are highly liked and extremely approachable by athletes and coaches. It's all part of the learning process to be open for questions and constructive criticism.

These officials typically come early and stay late to other games for additional learning from watching other people hone their craft. They tend to ask questions and value honest feedback on their own referee skills – always wanting someone with expertise to watch them work.

## *Type C:*
### *Novices with Closed Personalities*

In stark contrast to Type B, these officials can be spotted very early in the referee developmental programs, if you know what to look for.

Key signs of a problem in the making:

- Carries a know-it-all attitude
- Rarely shares (or asks) for advice from peers
- Doesn't say much to partners or coaches, but when they do, it typically is very negative.
- Many times is in the officiating profession strictly for the money and desires to extract from the game versus give back.
- Being a novice, spends little time learning the rules and mechanics of the game properly.
- Is extremely un-approachable by coaches because of their closed attitude toward people and their lack of game expertise.

Cadet and new officials that possess these traits are sometimes weeded out of the organizations, because their peer and coaches ratings reflect negative comments over a long period of time. But many times they slip through the cracks and stick around sucking the energy from the organization for their personal gain.

If a young official can see the benefits of changing their mind-set and move toward a Type B, they can be salvaged. Mentors and partners should look for these tell tale signs and make appropriate recommendations directly to the official, in the hope of putting them on the right path for success.

## Type D:
### Experts with Closed Personalities

Probably the worst combination of personality and knowledge is this veteran with a chip on their shoulder.

Similar to the novice, Type D's are extremely closed to any recommendations of improving their OWN game and will not give back anything to their peers to help advance a less experienced official. They will never ask for a post-game analysis with their crew and dismiss any supervisor's commentary on improving their game.

Coaches find Type D officials very arrogant and un-approachable. When they are confronted, even in a professional way, the official tends to escalate conversations into arguments which lead to unnecessary technical fouls and ejections. Many times these referees brag about "T-eeing" a coach or ejecting a player for minor infractions that could have been avoided by a more communicative approach.

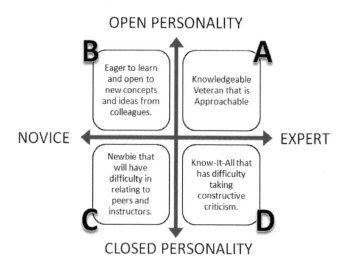

So what does this all mean?

## Recommendations

If you think that you are one of the CLOSED personalities, the focus should be on:

- Being more professional and approachable with coaches and players.
- Ask for feedback from colleagues. Every game (even pre-season / summer ball) should include a post-game question ... *"What could I (or we) have done better today?"* Ask the question and appreciate the honest feedback from your partners.
- Offer help to younger officials. Give some of your time to help newer officials learn the ropes of becoming a basketball referee. Ask first, before offering advice.
Something like ... *"I saw some areas today that you did very well and some that you could improve on. Would you like me to share these with you?"*
- Become a good listener and develop an open dialogue with peers and coaches. Think about better ways to ease controversy and diffuse difficult situations.

# Striving for Excellence

Officiating is like every other competitive endeavor you participate in. The painful reality is, **you are either getting better, or you are getting worse.**

The status quo is a false security blanket that some officials wrap themselves in who are not willing to do the necessary work to improve.

**Somewhere out in the vast basketball landscape, a dedicated official is working on their craft and when they meet a peer who is doing just enough to get by, there will be no mistaking the difference between the two.**

While the goal is always **personal skill building development on an ongoing basis to maximize your own ability,** officials must embrace the fact that games are stacked in a pyramid, with the quality of assignment improving as you journey up the narrowing pyramid.

Like it or not, you are competing for a coveted spot on the next rung of the officiating ladder in the pyramid, while at the same time trying to maintain firm footing on the perch you presently hold.

Admittedly, for the lion share of people who step onto a basketball court with a striped shirt and whistle, officiating will be an avocation that delivers more in the way of intangible benefits than it does financial rewards and notoriety.

While your love of the game will trump any cost analysis examination of the time, money and energy expended related to officiating, you should nevertheless bring the same passionate pursuit of excellence and professionalism to it as you do with your full-time vocation.

Some critical questions to answer in your pursuit of excellence:

> **Are you an official who communicates well with your assignors/supervisors and school officials? Do you take care of all of the necessary paperwork during the course of the season?**

Invariably it seems to be the same officials in every organization every year who are late paying their dues and their assessments. It is the same officials who don't follow the procedures for notifying schools and their partners for upcoming assignments and always seem to be scrambling to arrive on time for every game.

Be the official who is prompt with all of your paperwork and correspondence. Present yourself in attitude and appearance, at meetings, in conferences, and all public settings with an approach that represents the level of respect you want to be accorded.

There are exceptions to every rule, but you would be making a mistake to model yourself after the official with a quality game schedule who seems to wear boorish behavior, a disorganized lifestyle and sloppy appearance, as a badge of honor.

On game day, arrive neat and with a low profile. Your responsibility is to be courteous and professional with athletic directors and coaches during any pre-game interactions, but your goal is to earn their respect, not their friendship. Keep the conversations light and on point.

### Are you an official that always needs to be in the spotlight?

As the quality and quantity of your assignments improves, be mindful of your temperament and that your confidence doesn't drift to a level where your ego begins to negatively creep into your game.

Not every coach or player comment is a personal assault on your integrity. Let the game 'breathe' and look to diffuse situations, not ignite them.

Also, be careful not to be dismissive of a high school coach if you have advanced into the college ranks. The participants in your now less frequent scholastic assignments deserve your best attitude and effort. Don't let anyone be able to say, *"He acts like he's doing us a favor by being here."*

And consider for a moment where you and your partners decide to grab a post-game bite to eat. Picking a popular establishment near the game site will increase the chances you will be recognized by fans or coaches of the home team, which could lead to an awkward moment for everyone.

Ultimately, it will boil down to one question in your pursuit of excellence:

**Are you a person who is willing to do all that you can do, to be all that you can be?**

You have chosen a craft where half of the interested parties will be upset with every decision you make, so your satisfaction must be internally driven.

Identify the factors for excellence and advancement within your control, and work unceasingly at sharpening those skills. The external issues that are beyond your influence, you must begin to lessen your grip on.

When you understand the **"joy"** is literally in the **journey** of any pursuit worthy of your precious time, then you will be open to a level of personal satisfaction beyond what you have ever experienced.

The game within the game is first to be the best you can be, then put your fully-realized potential into the global basketball officiating marketplace, and embrace the results.

Get **beyond the rules** and go beyond what you ever thought possible!

# Officiating Resources

*Free Online Educational Resource for Officials*

INTERNATIONAL ASSOCIATION
OF APPROVED BASKETBALL OFFICIALS

## www.iaabo.org

*Through a worldwide organization of some 200 local "Boards"
spanning 38 States and 11 foreign counties, IAABO has been
the unparalleled and undisputed leader in worldwide training
of basketball officials for over 85 years.*